ANIMAL SCIENCE

SCIENCE 24/7

ANIMAL SCIENCE

CAR SCIENCE

COMPUTER SCIENCE

ENVIRONMENTAL SCIENCE

FASHION SCIENCE

FOOD SCIENCE

HEALTH SCIENCE

MUSIC SCIENCE

PHOTO SCIENCE

SPORTS SCIENCE

TRAVEL SCIENCE

SCIENCE 24/7

ANIMAL SCIENCE

JANE P. GARDNER

SCIENCE CONSULTANT:
RUSS LEWIN
SCIENCE AND MATH EDUCATOR

Mason Crest

Mason Crest
450 Parkway Drive, Suite D
Broomall, PA 19008
www.masoncrest.com

Printed and bound in the United States of America.

Series ISBN: 978-1-4222-3404-4
Hardback ISBN: 978-1-4222-3405-1
EBook ISBN: 978-1-4222-8489-6

3 5 7 9 8 6 4 2

Produced by Shoreline Publishing Group LLC
Santa Barbara, California
www.shorelinepublishing.com
Cover photo: Dreamstime.com/Photobac

Library of Congress Cataloging-in-Publication Data
Gardner, Jane P., author.
    Animal science / by Jane P. Gardner ; science consultant, Russ Lewin, science and math educator.
    pages cm. -- (Science 24/7)
    Audience: Grades 9-12
    Includes bibliographical references and index.
ISBN 978-1-4222-3405-1 (hardback) -- ISBN 978-1-4222-3404-4 (series) -- ISBN 978-1-4222-8489-6 (ebook) 1. Zoology--Miscellanea--Juvenile literature. 2. Ecology--Miscellanea--Juvenile literature.
I. Title.
QL49.G2485 2016
590--dc23
                              2015004962

IMPORTANT NOTICE
The science experiments, activities, and information described in this publication are for educational use only. The publisher is not responsible for any direct, indirect, incidental or consequential damages as a result of the uses or misuses of the techniques and information within.

Contents

Introduction 6

Chapter 1: Inheritance of Traits 8

Chapter 2: Flight 12

Chapter 3: Animal Behavior 16

Chapter 4: Adaptations 20

Chapter 5: Stay Warm 24

Chapter 6: Conservation 28

Chapter 7: Food Webs 32

Chapter 8: Temperature 36

Chapter 9: Conclusion: Concept Review 40

Find Out More 44

Series Glossary of Key Terms 45

Picture Credits 46

About the Author and Consultant 47

Index 48

KEY ICONS TO LOOK FOR

Words to Understand: These words with their easy-to-understand definitions will increase the reader's understanding of the text, while building vocabulary skills.

Sidebars: This boxed material within the main text allows readers to build knowledge, gain insights, explore possibilities, and broaden their perspectives by weaving together additional information to provide realistic and holistic perspectives.

Series Glossary of Key Terms: This back-of-the-book glossary contains terminology used throughout this series. Words found here increase the reader's ability to read and comprehend higher-level books and articles in this field.

INTRODUCTION

Science. Ugh! Is this the class you have to sit through in order to get to the cafeteria for lunch? Or, yeah! This is my favorite class! Whether you look forward to science or dread it, you can't escape it. Science is all around us all the time.

What do you think of when you think about science? People in lab coats peering anxiously through microscopes while scribbling notes? Giant telescopes scanning the universe for signs of life? Submersibles trolling the dark, cold, and lonely world of the deepest ocean? Yes, these are all science and things that scientists do to learn more about our planet, outer space, and the human body. But we are all scientists. Even you.

Science is about asking questions. Why do I have to eat my vegetables? Why does the sun set in the west? Why do cats purr and dogs bark? Why am I warmer when I wear a black jacket than when I wear a white one? These are all great questions. And these questions can be the start of something big . . . the start of scientific discovery.

1. **Observe:** Ask questions. What do you see in the world around you that you don't understand? What do you wish you knew more about? Remember, there is always more than one solution to a problem. This is the starting point for scientists—and it can be the starting point for you, too!

    Enrique took a slice of bread out of the package and discovered there was mold on it. "Again?" he complained. "This is the second time this all-natural bread I bought turned moldy before I could finish it. I wonder why."

2. **Research:** Find out what you can about the observation you have made. The more information you learn about your observation, the better you will understand which questions really need to be answered.

    Enrique researched the term "all-natural" as it applied to his bread. He discovered that it meant that no preservatives were used. Some breads contain preservatives, which are used to "maintain freshness." Enrique wondered if it was the lack of preservatives that was allowing his bread to grow mold.

3. **Predict:** Consider what might happen if you were to design an experiment based on your research. What do you think you would find?

    Enrique thought that maybe it was the lack of preservatives in his bread that was causing the mold. He predicted that bread containing preservatives would last longer than "all-natural" breads.

4. **Develop a Hypothesis:** A hypothesis is a possible answer or solution to a scientific problem. Sometimes, they are written as an "if-then" statement. For example, "If I get a good night's sleep, then I will do well on the test tomorrow." This is not a fact; there is no guarantee that the hypothesis is correct. But it is a statement that can be tested with an experiment. And then, if necessary, revised once the experiment has been done.

Enrique thinks that he knows what is going on. He figures that the preservatives in the bread are what keeps it from getting moldy. His working hypothesis is "If bread contains preservatives, it will not grow mold." He is now ready to test his hypothesis.

5. **Design an Experiment:** An experiment is designed to test a hypothesis. It is important when designing an experiment to look at all the variables. Variables are the factors that will change in the experiment. Some variables will be independent—these won't change. Others are dependent and will change as the experiment progresses. A control is necessary too. This is a constant throughout the experiment against which results can be compared.

Enrique plans his experiment. He chooses two slices of his bread, and two slices of the bread with preservatives. He uses a small kitchen scale to ensure that the slices are approximately the same weight. He places a slice of each on the windowsill where they will receive the same amount of sunlight. He places the other two slices in a dark cupboard. He checks on his bread every day for a week. He finds that his bread gets mold in both places while the bread with preservatives starts to grow a little mold in the sunshine but none in the cupboard.

6. **Revise the hypothesis:** Sometimes the result of your experiment will show that the original hypothesis is incorrect. That is okay! Science is all about taking risks, making mistakes, and learning from them. Rewriting a hypothesis after examining the data is what this is all about.

Enrique realized it may be more than the preservatives that prevents mold. Keeping the bread out of the sunlight and in a dark place will help preserve it, even without preservatives. He has decided to buy smaller quantities of bread now, and keep it in the cupboard.

This book has activities for you to try at the end of each chapter. They are meant to be fun, and teach you a little bit at the same time. Sometimes, you'll be asked to design your own experiment. Think back to Enrique's experience when you start designing your own. And remember—science is about being curious, being patient, and not being afraid of saying you made a mistake. There are always other experiments to be done!

1
INHERITANCE OF TRAITS

Jesse and his friend, Gabriella, headed to their local pet store, which is called "All Pets, All the Time." Jesse needed to buy crickets to feed his pet gecko and liked the owner, Mr. Wei. Mr. Wei is very nice and doesn't mind if the kids browse in the store for a long time.

The bell over the door chimed, announcing their arrival. An old golden retriever rose out of a dog bed next to the counter to meet them. A large blue bird swooped to a roost over the cash register. They heard a dog barking and crickets chirping in the background. And next to them was a large display of woven bracelets in front of a poster of elephants and rhinos.

"Kittens!" exclaimed Gabriella. She rushed over to where a mother cat and her eight kittens were playing and lounging in a large enclosure. Jesse walked over to take a look at them as well.

"Look at them," he said. "They are so different. Tiger stripes, calico, and look at that solid black one. Why is there only one mother cat here?"

Mr. Wei came up behind them and picked up the large cat with tiger stripes and an orange face. "This is the mother. She was found near a dumpster last week with all these babies."

Gabriella looked up. "How could one mother cat have kittens with so many different patterns?"

Mr. Wei smiled at her. "Take a look at them. Are they really that different?" Then he went to help another customer who was ready to pay.

Jesse and Gabriella turned back to the kittens. "Well, the mother is a tabby cat," Jesse said. "Black, orange, and white spots with some brown blotches."

"Right, and some of the kittens have those same colors," added Gabriella.

They took a closer look at the kittens. "Actually, they all have small tufts of hair off their ears, just like their mother," said Jesse.

"You're right, Jesse. And the ears are all rounded on top, not pointed like on my cat at home."

Jesse and Gabriella remembered what they had learned in science class. Organisms display traits. Traits include things like eye color in humans, the shape of ears or the color of fur in kittens, and seed shape or stem height in plants. Traits are determined by the genes of an individual organism. Individuals get their genes from their parents. Sometimes individuals display the same traits as their parents, sometimes they don't.

Genes are made of two parts called alleles [ul-LEELS]. Some alleles are dominant—this allele has the trait that will always appear if it is in the gene. Others are recessive—it is hidden when there is a dominant allele around.

Gabriella turned to her friend. "Jesse, what color are your eyes?"

"Brown."

"What about your parents?"

"Umm. My mom has brown eyes. And my dad has blue eyes."

"And I have brown eyes, as do both of my parents. Remember what we learned? Brown eyes are dominant; the allele brown always shows through."

Jesse knew what she was talking about and piped in,

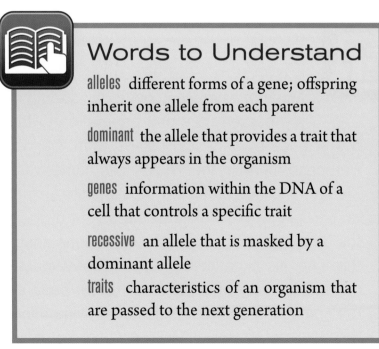

Words to Understand

alleles different forms of a gene; offspring inherit one allele from each parent

dominant the allele that provides a trait that always appears in the organism

genes information within the DNA of a cell that controls a specific trait

recessive an allele that is masked by a dominant allele

traits characteristics of an organism that are passed to the next generation

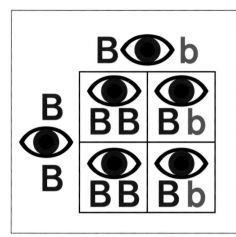

This Punnett square shows how Jesse and Gabriella can't have blue eyes. There would need to be a "b-b" pair for that to happen.

"And blue is recessive." He pulled a piece of a paper and pencil out of his backpack. "Punnett squares—remember these?"

Drawing a box and splitting it in two, he continued.

"My dad has blue eyes. The only way he can have blue eyes is if he has two recessive alleles. So that is lower case b and lower case b."

Gabriella continued. "And your mom has brown eyes. So she has at least a dominant gene—capital B. We don't know for sure what the other allele is, do we?"

Jesse thought for a moment. "Well, both my grandparents have brown eyes, too."

"Okay," said Gabriella. "Then let's assume she has two dominant alleles—BB."

The kids completed the Punnett square using Jesse's parents. They saw no "b-b" combinations. "Huh. Look at that. There is no way my brother or I could have had blue eyes."

"Right, and it looks as if these kittens are in the same boat. Their mother had a dominant allele for tufted ears. All the kittens show it. So we can probably assume that the mother has two dominant alleles. It doesn't even matter what the father's ears looked like."

Gregor Mendel

Much of what we know today about how traits are passed from one generation to the next—the science of genetics—comes from the work of a European monk in the 1800s. His name was Gregor Mendel and he conducted thousands of experiments on pea plants. He looked at the height of their stems,

the arrangement of their flowers, and the shape of the pea pods and seeds. At the time, his experiments didn't receive much attention. But the world would eventually know what his ideas about peas and genetics could mean for the understanding of the genetics of all living things!

Try It Yourself

What did the kittens' parents look like?

Sometimes it is possible to trace the traits of the parents by looking at the offspring. What if you could make your own "paper pet" and give it some unique and wacky traits. What would its parents have looked like?

Materials:

Construction paper

Scissors

Stickers of various shapes, sizes, and colors

Markers, colored pencils

1. Decide on four unique traits you want your "pet" to have. Will it have long legs or short legs? Curly fur or long fur? Pointed ears or rounded ears? List the traits that you will highlight in your pet.

2. Indicate on the list whether or not the specific trait is dominant or recessive.

3. Create your pet using the materials available.

4. Draw Punnett squares for at least two of the traits your pet has—one recessive and one dominant. What traits did its parents have? What alleles made up those traits? Remember, traits come from the parents equally.

2
FLIGHT

Gabriella let out a shriek as Rocco, the blue and gold macaw, swooped down over her head to land on a perch hanging from the ceiling.

"Whoa! Did you see that thing fly?"

Rocco took off again, swooping up and over tall shelves and down the aisles, soaring and flapping his big blue wings. "How does he do that?" Gabriella cried out.

Tyrell, the manager of the bird collection at the store, came over with Rocco sitting on his shoulder. "It's a matter of simple physics."

Jesse looked doubtful. "Is there really any such thing as *simple* physics?"

Tyrell laughed. "Sure there is. Here, take Rocco and I'll show you something."

Placing the big macaw on

Words to Understand

lift the difference in pressure between the top of a bird, or airplane, wing and the bottom, enabling flight to occur

Jesse's shoulder, Tyrell led the kids into the back room. Glancing uncertainly at the bird on his shoulder, Jesse followed Gabriella.

Tyrell pulled a book out of a desk drawer. "I like to read during my lunch break." Pulling out the strip of paper he used as a bookmark, he continued, "What do you think will happen if I blow across this paper?"

Gabriella looked at the book and the strip of paper. "I bet it flaps in the wind you create with your breath."

"Let's see." As Tyrell gently blew across the top of the paper, the kids were surprised to see the paper rise. Tyrell blew even harder and the paper came to a horizontal position and flapped until he stopped blowing.

Putting the book down, Tyrell said with a smile. "And that is why Rocco, other birds, and airplanes can fly."

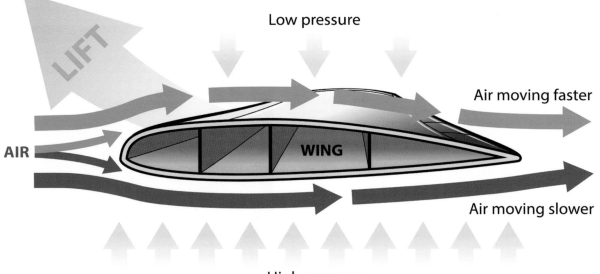

LIFT

Low pressure

Air moving faster

AIR

WING

Air moving slower

High pressure

The horizontal arrows show air moving over the wing.
When the pressure over the wing goes down, lift is created.

"Huh?" Jesse said. "What does that have to do with Rocco flying?"

"It's a physical property called 'lift.' Rocco's wings, like a wing of an airplane, are designed to produce an upward force, called lift. See how the wing is slanted a little? Air moving over the top of the wing flows faster than the air moving along the bottom of the wing. This means the air flowing over the top of the wing exerts less pressure than the air moving along the bottom. This creates an upward motion."

"Oh! I get it. Just like when you blew on the paper. The air you were blowing was moving faster than the air on the underside of the paper. There was less pressure on the top, so it is almost like the air on the bottom side of the paper pushed it up."

"Right! And that is how our friend Rocco here flies too." Tyrell clapped his hands and Rocco lifted up off of Jesse's shoulder and flew to his outstretched hand.

Bernoulli's Principle

Why does the air flowing over the top of the slanted wing move faster? And how does that result in a lower pressure? The answer to these questions can be found in Bernoulli's Principle. This says that as the speed of a fluid in motion (in this case, the air) increases, then the pressure in that fluid decreases. Bernoulli's principle was first discovered in the 1700s by a scientist in Switzerland named Daniel Bernoulli, who found that fluids in motion behave differently than fluids at rest.

Try It Yourself

Make your own paper bird.

Some birds soar on winds high up in the sky. Other birds flap their wings and flutter from branch to branch. What do their wings look like? Design your own "bird" and see how it flies.

Materials:

Drinking straws

Tape

Heavy weight paper or very thin cardboard

1. Decide if you want to make a paper airplane shaped like a bird that soars, such as a hawk, or one that flaps its wings more, like a robin.

2. Check out the Internet or other resources to find pictures of the bird you want to replicate. Take note of their wing shapes.

3. Use the materials listed to make a paper airplane. Be sure to keep in mind the basics behind the idea of lift.

4. If possible, toss your paper airplane along the length of the gymnasium or auditorium to observe its flight patterns. Make adjustments to your design as needed.

3

ANIMAL BEHAVIOR

"Huh. Look at that. She did it again." Gabriella figured she was talking to herself; she knew that Jesse was too busy checking out the snakes in the reptile cage.

"What? Who are you talking to?" Maybe he was paying attention.

"Watch Mr. Wei's dog, Ginger," Gabriella said. "Every time a customer comes in, she pulls herself up out of her bed and goes to greet the new person. Then she goes back to her bed behind the counter and gets all settled in again. When the door opens, she does the whole thing over. I've been watching her. This has happened five times since we've been standing here looking at these snakes."

Jesse looked away from a python, which was slowly swallowing a frozen mouse.

"Do the customers pat her on the head?"

"Uh . . . yeah. I think most of them do."

"If you got pat on the head each time someone came in," laughed Jesse, "wouldn't you go greet them, too?" He turned back to the snake.

"Well, I don't know if I would necessarily, but I can see why the dog would like that." Moving away from the reptile cages, Gabriella found an empty chair to sit down and watch the dog's behavior.

Over the next ten minutes or so, she watched Ginger. Every time the bell over the door chimed, the dog would get out of her bed and walk to greet the customer. After receiving a pat on the head, most of the time, the dog would return to her bed.

"This is a very interesting behavior that Ginger is showing," Gabriella thought to herself. She remembered what she had learned in science class. Some behaviors are done by instinct. These are done by an animal without practice or experience—and they are done right the first time. For example, a bird isn't taught to build a nest—they just are born knowing how to do it.

But Gabriella realized that Mr. Wei's dog wasn't born knowing to get up from her bed and walk to new customers—she had to learn it. Ginger was showing a specific type of learning

Pavlovian Response

Does the aroma of food cooking sometimes make your mouth water? You could be conditioned to react that way. In the 1900s, a scientist from Russia named Ivan Pavlov did a series of experiments on a dog. He conditioned the dog to salivate when a bell was rung. Pavlov rang a bell each time he fed his dog over a couple of weeks. By the end, the dog would salivate whenever it heard the bell ring, even if there was no food available. This is known as a Pavlovian response—and a hungry dog!

called **conditioning**. The dog knew that the sound of the doorbell most likely meant that someone was coming in. And if Ginger got up to greet the person, then she was likely to get a pat on the head. Something good would happen if she responded to the bell. She learned this over time; she was conditioned to this behavior.

Mice can be trained using conditioning to make their way through a maze, evidence of their ability to learn.

Try It Yourself!

Think you could train an animal using conditioning?

Design an experiment that you think would work. Suppose you had two pet mice. You wanted to see if they could follow a maze. One mouse gets a treat at the end of its maze. The other doesn't. What would your experiment look like?

Suggested Materials:
Paper
Pencil

1. Devise your hypothesis.

2. What is your procedure? List the steps.

3. How many trials will you do? What is your controlled variable? Your independent variable?

4. Predict what your results will be.

5. Explain what you think you would see.

6. Draw a conclusion.

Note: If you happen to have a mouse for a pet, try this out! Or try a similar experiment on your cat, dog, or pet lizard. Just be sure to be kind and gentle to the pet. Have fun!

4
ADAPTATIONS

Jesse and Gabriella stood in front of the display of tanks. Inside were dozens of animals: toads, frogs, salamanders, snakes, lizards, and turtles. Some were crawling on branches or hiding under logs while others were partially submerged in small pools of water. The sign hanging over the displays read "Reptiles and Amphibians of the World."

Gabriella shook her head, "I can never remember the difference between reptiles and amphibians."

"Maybe I can help." Mr. Wei's assistant Mia came out from behind the display cases with a large boa constrictor wrapped around her neck like a scarf. "At first glance, they seem very similar. Lots of people get them confused." She pointed to a tank with some tree frogs on display. "What differences do you see between those frogs and Simba here?" she asked, pointing to the boa constrictor around her neck.

Reaching a cautious hand out to pet the snake, Jesse said, "Well, Simba's skin is dry, thick, and scaly. Those frogs look damp. And from what I know about frogs, they do need to stay moist."

"That's exactly right!" said Mia. "The skin of the amphibians is thin and has to be moist. These animals have adapted to different environments. Also, reptile skin is made of scales, while amphibian skin is smooth. That's because the reptiles molt, or shed their skin as they grow. The scales make that process easier. Amphibians don't molt, so their skin can grow as their body grows.

Also, water is important to the life cycle of an amphibian, like the frogs here. Amphibians lay their eggs in water and spend the early part of their lives in water. Adults live on land, but will return to the water to lay their eggs.

"But reptiles don't do that. They lay their eggs on land. Their eggs have a thick shell that lets oxygen into the egg. The egg has fluids and a yolk to keep the embryo cushioned, safe, and fed while in the egg. These eggs don't need to be in the water because the egg is designed to conserve water."

"That sounds a little bit like a chicken egg," Gabriella realized.

"Yes, it does. But instead of sitting on their eggs, like a hen does, to keep them warm, a reptile will usually cover their eggs in sand and wait for the sun to warm them."

"That's right! One time we were on the beach and saw turtles laying eggs in the sand."

These frogs began life as tadpoles, animals that are adapted to live in water.

Words to Understand

amphibian a cold-blooded organism who lives in the water during its early life and then on land as an adult

reptile a cold-blooded animal that lays eggs on land and has dry, scaly skin

Dinosaurs

Do you think reptiles are small, shy animals that hide under rocks? Think again. If you could travel back in time, to around 245 million years ago, you'd encounter some very, very big reptiles. Dinosaurs and their relatives were reptiles. In fact, the Mesozoic era from 245 to 66 million years ago was known as The Age of the Reptiles.

"In fact," added Mia, "only a tiny handful of reptiles stick around to help their young grow. Most simply leave the eggs to hatch on their own. The baby reptiles have to feed themselves as soon as they are born. That's another reason they bury the eggs . . . to protect them from animals who would eat the eggs."

"That's right," said Gabriella. "I remember reading about people who help keep those sea turtle eggs in the sand safe. They put up barriers to keep dogs and other animals from digging up the eggs. Sometimes Mother Nature needs our help, too!"

As they admired the beauty of the frogs and as Simba curled around Mia's arm, Mia added, "Each kind of animal adapted over time to create the best conditions for future generations."

Try It Yourself!

The eggs of a reptile are similar in many ways to a chicken's egg. Learn more about how these eggs are adapted for survival on land by taking a closer look at a chicken's egg.

Science Safety: Be sure to clean up all spills. <u>Wash your hands thoroughly</u> after completing this activity. Do not eat anything in this activity.

Suggested Materials

Chicken egg, raw

Paper towels

Sharp knife or pointed scissors

Magnifying glass or microscope

Shallow dish or bowl

1. Get a raw chicken's egg and place it in a "nest" of paper towels. Describe the outermost part of the shell.

2. Carefully tap the shell with the scissors or knife to break a small hole in the shell. Insert the knife or scissors into the small hole and cut a large hole in the egg.

3. Pour the contents of the egg into the small bowl, taking care not to break the yolk.

4. Use the magnifying glass to look at the egg shell. What do you see?

5. How do you think the evolution of the hard egg shell helped reptiles live on land?

6. Continue to use the magnifying glass to examine the egg yolk. What does this look like?

7. The yolk is the food for the developing embryo. If this egg was fertilized and an embryo was inside, what would you expect the yolk to look like when the egg hatched?

8. Examine the "white" of the egg. This is the clear, liquid part of the egg. What do you think the function of this part of the egg is?

5
STAY WARM

Gabriella giggled, "Hey, Jesse. Do you think I should get one of these pink sweaters for Thunder?" She was standing in front of a display of sweaters, coats, and booties for small dogs.

Picking up a tiny sweater with sequins, Jesse smiled, "I don't think that a huge German shepherd like Thunder would fit into this!"

Gabriella read what was written on the poster over the display of dog supplies.

" 'Made with real alpaca wool.' Wow. This is high quality stuff. I have a pair of mittens made of alpaca wool my aunt got me in Peru. They are by far the warmest mittens ever."

Glancing at the photo of the alpacas in the Andes mountains, Jesse said, "Wow. No wonder those mittens are so warm. Look at how cold it must be on top of those mountains. Those alpacas must have some very thick fur."

"They've adapted to that environment. Remember what we learned about other animals that live where it is cold? Polar bears, for example, have black skin under their white fur. The black skin absorbs the sun's energy to help keep it warm. They have a thick undercoating of fur, and some of it is even hollow, which helps insulate it."

"That's right! In fact, polar bears often get too warm and move slowly on land so they don't overheat. Who would think it could get too cold up at the North Pole?"

Fingering the dog coat again, Gabriella said "This alpaca fur must provide good insulation, too. That is why it can keep the animals warm, and keep us warm."

Jesse continued "I remember learning other things about animals in the Arctic and their adaptations to the cold. Wolves in the Arctic look slightly different from the wolves elsewhere. Their legs are a little bit shorter, their ears are smaller, and their muzzle is shorter. Animals lose heat through their ears, on the underside of their belly, and off their muzzle. These small differences in the arctic wolves helps them survive the long, cold, harsh winter."

"And don't forget about the blubber." Gabriella added "Many of the animals in the Arctic have a thick layer of blubber under their skin. Marine mammals such as whales have a layer of blubber over their entire body except for their fins and flippers. Blubber insulates the animal while providing energy, too!"

Thanks to insulation and dark skin, polar bears survive the cold.

Try it Yourself!

How do animals, like sheep or alpaca, or polar bears, stay out in the cold and wet weather without freezing? Do wool socks or wool mittens really keep you warm and dry? Find out in this short experiment!

Suggested Materials:
Pair of wool socks or mittens
2 plastic cups, with lid
Thermometers
Hot tap water

1. Soak one sock or mitten in room temperature tap water. Wring it out so that it is still damp but not dripping.

2. Carefully place a plastic cup inside each sock or mitten. Fold down the top so you can access the cup easily.

3. Pour hot tap water into each cup and carefully place the top on them. Insert a thermometer through the hole for the straw in each one.

4. Unroll the sock or mitten so that it covers the top of the cup, but make sure you can still read the thermometer.

5. Measure the temperature of each container. Then, measure the temperature in each container every five minutes for at least 20 minutes.

6. What did you find?

7. What does this say about wool? Does it keep you warm even when wet?

8. Why do you think animals such as mountain goats or sheep are adapted for life in cold environments?

6
CONSERVATION

S top the Killing. Stop the Trading," read Jesse while looking at another poster, this one showing a herd of African elephants. "Wow! Gabriella, look at this."

Gabriella leaned in to read more. " 'Elephants in Africa and Asia are being killed for their ivory tusks!' How horrible."

They read the rest of the poster. They learned that there is an underground, illegal, and unfortunately profitable business in Africa and Asia that deals with poaching ivory. Poaching is the illegal hunting of animals. "Listen to this! Things like piano keys and pool table balls are made from ivory. I think I've seen fancy chess sets in the museum made of ivory, too!"

"I wonder how much ivory you get from one elephant."

Reading the fine print on the poster, Jesse found the answer. " 'One elephant tusk can have as much as 10 kilograms of ivory.' That's just over 22 pounds. For only one tusk! Whoa. That is a lot of ivory from one elephant."

"I know, Jesse, but look." Gabriella was pointing to another photo. It showed a dead elephant on the ground, its tusks cut off, the animal left to rot in the hot sun. "They aren't even using the elephant for meat or any other purpose.

"It looks like they are just killing them for their tusks. And then they move to the next elephant."

"Look at this." Gabriella found another story on the pamphlets. "Poachers also kill sharks for their fins. You know, as in shark fin soup. This article talks about how this is affecting the shark population and the entire ocean ecosystem!"

Jesse was curious. "How can a few sharks affect the whole ocean?"

"Well, the shark is one of the top predators. Without the sharks, the population of their prey is growing. This impacts the source of food in the area. The whole balance is upset."

Jesse kept reading. "Poaching is even hurting the economy in some places. Apparently, shark safaris are huge for tourists. Killing a shark gets the poacher the money for the fin but that's a

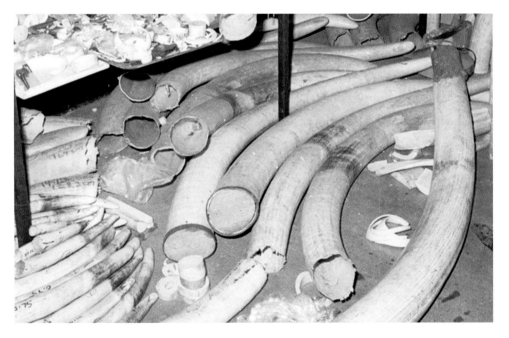

Police try to capture poachers and take away the stolen ivory.

Rhino Poaching

A rhino is safe from ivory poachers, because their horns are not made of ivory. In the past, it was believed that they were made of hair but recent studies by scientists at Ohio University found that the horns are made of a material similar to horse hooves. However, rhinos are still poached; their horns are believed in some cultures to have magic powers and are used in carvings. In some places, biologists capture the rhinos and remove most of their horn surgically. It is hoped that the animals won't be killed by poaches if they have no horn to steal.

one-time deal. Only the poacher benefits. But if the shark is left in the ocean, then many people benefit—the tour guide, boat driver, and the people who run the restaurants and hotels in the area. The impact of poaching sharks can be felt in the ocean and on land!"

Gabriella sighed. "I bet poaching elephants has just as much impact on the ecosystems in Africa and Asia."

Jesse dug into his pocket for some money. He put it into a donation box below the poster. "I'm sure it does."

Try It Yourself!

Want to help stop elephant poaching? The best way is to inform others—get the word out about the dangers of buying products made of ivory. Show people how it is not just the elephants that are in danger from this practice, but the entire ecosystem!

Suggested Materials:

Internet access

Poster board or construction paper

Markers, colored pencils

Go online! Research elephant poaching in Africa and the impact it has on the elephant population and the ecosystem in general. Create an informative pamphlet or poster to inform others. Include the following:

- Facts about the status of the elephant population
- Information about who is poaching and where they are selling the ivory
- Products made of ivory and the market for them
- Impacts on the ecosystem
- Impacts on humans

Photos, maps, and statistics can help give your pamphlet or poster more impact!

7
FOOD WEBS

In the middle of the pet store, Mr. Wei had put up a large enclosure. Part terrarium, part animal cage it was home to a variety of plants, mushrooms, and small animals. From where he was standing, Jesse could see grasshoppers, butterflies, and a large, brown bug that looked very much like a stick.

Mr. Wei walked over with a spray bottle and some pieces of lettuce. "I need to keep the plants moist in here," he explained. "And someone in here really likes lettuce. I'm not sure which animal it is, but they eat it up pretty quick."

After Mr. Wei leaves, Jesse takes a closer look at the organisms within the enclosure. He notices a few things. There is a grasshopper nibbling on the plants on the bottom of the cage. *"I wonder if that's who is eating the lettuce."* One of the butterflies flies out from under the pile of rocks in one corner. A few carpenter ants are digging a hole in the soil and Jesse sees a few other ants carrying pieces of green lettuce across the ground. *"Nope, it's the ants!"* The stick bug is camouflaged on a branch, soaking up the warmth of the heat lamp.

Gabriella comes over to take a look, too. "It's one giant food web."

"That's just what I was thinking," Jesse said. "I have seen two food chains at work already."

"Oh yeah. I forgot that you could break down a food web into different interconnected food chains."

Jesse pointed to the ants. "Look at those ants. They are digging in the soil. I think they are eating the bacteria that live there. And they are ripping parts of the leaves off the plants and the lettuce that Mr. Wei put in there."

"And imagine what would happen if we dropped another animal in there. What if we added a frog in there?"

"The frog would probably love to get its tongue on those grasshoppers."

"Wow," Gabriella said, "It's a lot easier to trace a food web when you can actually see it at work. The energy from the plants is being transferred to the grasshopper which would go to the frog if we added it in there."

A colony of ants is part of the food webs in many ecosystems.

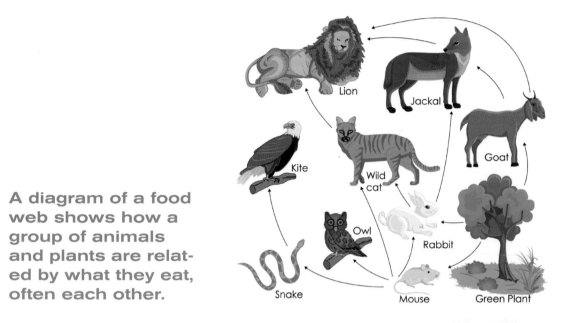

A diagram of a food web shows how a group of animals and plants are related by what they eat, often each other.

Labels in diagram: Lion, Jackal, Goat, Kite, Wild cat, Rabbit, Owl, Snake, Mouse, Green Plant

"And don't forget the sun. The plants get their energy from the sun, or maybe from that heat lamp there. Either way, the energy has to start somewhere."

"Look at that butterfly," Gabriella said, pointing to a beautiful blue-winged creature. "It keeps returning to those rocks. I bet it is using the rocks to hide, or to lay its eggs or something. Whatever it is doing there, the butterfly sure is interacting with the rocks."

"Remember what we learned, Gabriella. Living organisms will interact with both other living things and nonliving things in their environment. Just like the ants are using the soil to build their homes and store their food."

Jesse nodded his head. "Yep. We could make this display a lot more interesting if we could add a few frogs and some of those snakes over there!"

Ecosystems Everywhere

Not every environment or food web requires the sun. Deep, deep in the ocean the sunlight doesn't reach the bottom of the ocean floor. But a thriving ecosystem of organisms lives there. The organisms are near hydrothermal vents, openings in the ocean floor from which mineral-rich and magma-warmed water enters the ocean. Bacteria living there get their energy from the chemicals in the water and form the basis of the food chain for the organisms in the area.

Try It Yourself!

Take a walk in a local park or just sit in your backyard. If you are observant and patient, you will most likely be able to identify at least one food web at work there. What organisms are eating which other ones? What happens when an organism in this environment dies? Be sure to check out the producers, consumers, and decomposers in the food web.

Suggested Materials:
Poster board
Colored pencils, markers
Different colored yarn

1. Identify at least four different producers and four different primary and secondary consumers in your environment. What are they?

2. Identify the source of energy in your food web.

3. What decomposers are working here? How do you know?

4. Draw the interactions between these organisms on the poster board. Use yarn to represent the flow of energy from the producers to the primary consumers to the secondary consumers.

8
TEMPERATURE

"Mr. Wei, can I please get two dozen large crickets?" Jesse finally was getting around to the purpose of his trip to the pet store.

"Coming right up. How is your gecko these days?"

"He's doing well. He seems to be eating a lot more lately. I think it's probably because it's warmer now. He seemed to really slow down during the winter."

Mr. Wei continued to count the fast-moving crickets crawling around in the clear plastic bag. "Well, that is what happens with cold-blooded reptiles." Snapping the rubber band used to seal the bag, he handed it to Jesse. "Cold temperatures don't only affect reptiles, you know. Have you noticed a difference in your crickets, too?"

Jesse held up the bag and looked at the insects squirming and crawling over each other. "No, not really."

"Let me help with this." Mia came over. She was the reptile expert in the store.

"As you may know, crickets and other insects are cold-blooded. Basically, they take on the temperature of their surroundings. Where does your gecko hang out on chilly days, Jesse?"

Jesse thought for a minute. "He loves to sit under the heat lamp on top of his rock."

"Exactly! He is soaking up the warmth of the heat lamp. Cold-blooded organisms have no way to regulate their body temperature internally. Reptiles, insects, and other cold-blooded organisms need to seek shade if they are too hot and seek the sun if they are too cold."

Gabriella spoke up. "So, I'm guessing that a warm-blooded organism does have the ability to regulate their temperature, no matter what is going on outside."

"Yep. That's what happens."

Jesse looked at his bag of squirming crickets again. "What does this all have to do with crickets?"

"Well, it is a matter of chemistry and temperature," said Mia. "The chirping noise you hear is actually made by the male crickets. They rub their wings together. One wing has a ridge on it called a 'scraper' while the other wing has wrinkles called 'files.' The cricket will run the scraper along the files to make that noise. In warm temperatures, the crickets have more energy. This makes them more active and therefore they are noisier."

Gabriella stared at the crickets in the bag. "Why do they do that exactly?"

"They are communicating. They may be warning other crickets of danger, or telling another male to stay away, or they may be trying to attract a female. But whatever the reason, the fact that these cold-blooded insects are noisier in the summer explains why many people think of summer evenings when they hear crickets chirp."

Jesse laughed. "It is like a summer evening every day at my house with all these crickets!"

Crickets "sing" a song that unique to each individual species.

Summer Buzzin'

Have you ever heard a cicada? If you have, you probably wouldn't forget it. These insects are the noisiest insects anywhere. One male can make a noise of over 100 decibels. A jet airplane traveling 1000 feet in the air only makes a noise of 90 decibels! Now imagine thousands of male cicadas making that same noise.

Every 13 to 17 years, some species emerge from underground, make a huge racket, mate, and then lay eggs in the ground. That is the entire life cycle. But they sure make a lot of noise while they are here.

Try It Yourself!

Years ago, a book called *The Farmers' Almanac* published an equation which can be used to find the approximate temperature based on the number of cricket chirps. To find the approximate temperature in degrees Fahrenheit, count the number of chirps for 14 seconds and then add 40 to that number. This will give you approximately the correct temperature.

Is this accurate? Try it yourself and see.

Suggested Materials

Stopwatch

Outdoor thermometer

Outdoor crickets or purchased from pet store

Evening between 55 and 100 degrees F

1. Record the outside temperature.

Be sure to record your temperature in degrees Fahrenheit

2. Bring your crickets outside or sit in a yard where you can hear the crickets. Sit quietly for a while to get used to the noises. See if you can identify the chirp of one particular cricket.

3. Using the stopwatch, count the number of chirps that cricket makes in 14 seconds. How many was it? Make sure that you are counting the chirps of one individual cricket.

4. Repeat Step 3 three more times. Why is that important?

5. Take the average of the four counts. What was the average number of chirps?

6. Add 40 to that average number. What is the approximate temperature, according to the crickets?

7. How does this compare with the actual temperature you measured with the thermometer?

8. What would you expect to find if the temperatures were warmer? Or cooler? Explain.

9
CONCLUSION

Animal Science. There is so much about animals that focuses on science. Science helps explain why animals behave in certain ways. It helps explain how animals change and adapt to their surroundings and environment. And science even helps us predict the temperature based on cricket chirps.

And, as Jesse and Gabriella learned, there are many aspects of an animal's life and environment which can help or hinder its chance for survival. Animals have adaptations that help them fly, or stay warm in extreme environments, or blend into their surroundings. But, as is the case with the elephants that Jesse and Gabriella learned about, animal survival often hinges on human behavior as well.

Think about this. There are an estimated 7.7 million species of animals on Earth. But those are the ones that have been discovered. Some scientists estimate that there are millions more that have not been discovered and classified. And unfortunately, between 0.01% and 0.1% of those species will go extinct this year. That's between 77,000 and 770,000 species each year!

You have probably read a lot about global warming and climate change and other environmental ills in the world. Water pollution, air pollution, greenhouse gases. These are all real environmental concerns. And there is much out there describing how this affects our lives and future. Our lives as human beings. But what about the animals in the world? How are these climatic changes and environmental issues affecting them? Perhaps in ways we aren't thinking enough about.

Here's one last activity for you to try. Do a quick Internet search about the impact of some of the larger oil spills have historically had on the wildlife in the area. You will be sure to find photographs of sea birds covered in sticky, black oil. Of particular danger from these spills are diving birds, like the laughing gull, brown pelican, and northern gannet. In fact, these species were most affected by the 2011 oil spill in the Gulf of Mexico.

So, what happens to the birds when they are exposed to the oil? And what can be done about it? Try this activity to find out what happens to their feathers. Collect a bird feather from a chicken or a pet bird. Examine it with a magnifying glass or under a microscope. Notice how

Oil spills can cause great damage to birds caught in the goo.

When humans make a mess, it's up to us to help clean it up.

you can run your finger along the feather and disrupt the individual parts and then you can rearrange them into a smooth pattern again. Now, place a drop of vegetable oil on the feather and rub it in. This is how the bird would try to clean oil off its feathers. What happens now when you try to rearrange the parts of the feather? Look at the oil spot with the magnifying glass or through the microscope. What does it look like? What do you think this will do to the bird if all its feathers were covered in oil?

The waterproofing ability of a seabird's feathers is essential to its survival. As you can see, exposure to oil alters the structure of a feather. This is just one small example of how our actions and decisions we make can impact the animal world. What can you do? Share what you have discovered in this book with your friends and family. Encourage them to become animal lovers and protectors as well.

Animal Science 24–7: Concept Review

Chapter 1
How is it possible that kittens in the same litter have a variety of colors and patterns? Jesse and Gabriella learned about how traits are passed from parents to offspring.

Chapter 2
Birds glide through the air thanks to the shape of their wings and the pressure of the air moving around those wings.

Chapter 3
Some behaviors are learned; others are instinctual. This chapter covered the different reasons behind animal behaviors.

Chapter 4
Animals are adapted to their environments. Their characteristics help them survive and thrive in the places they live.

Chapter 5
Living in a cold environment requires some serious insulation. This chapter explored some of the adaptations used by animals living in the tundra to survive.

Chapter 6
Species of animals are going extinct at an alarming rate. Efforts to protect the animals and the ecosystems they are part of became a focus for Jesse and Gabriella.

Chapter 7
Living things within an ecosystem do not live in isolation. There is a dependence among the organisms there, which can be traced on a food web.

Chapter 8
Animals interact with their surroundings in ways that humans can't. This chapter explored how something as simple as crickets chirping can provide information about the environment.

Find Out More

Books

Derocher, Andrew E. Polar Bears: *A Complete Guide to Their Biology and Behavior.* Baltimore: Johns Hopkins University Press, 2012.

Morell, Virginia. *Animal Wise: How We Know Animals Think and Feel.* New York: Broadway Books, 2014.

Scardina, Julie and Jeff Flocken. *Wildlife Heroes: 40 Leading Conservationists and the Animals They Are Committed to Saving.* Philadelphia: Running Press, 2012.

Spelman, Lucy. *National Geographic Animal Encyclopedia.* Washington, D.C.: National Geographic Books, 2012.

Zeligs, Jennifer. *Animal Training 101: The Complete and Practical Guide to the Art and Science of Behavior Modification.* Minneapolis: Mill City Press, 2014.

Web Sites

www.nationalzoo.si.edu
The Web site of the National Zoo in Washington, D.C. boasts an array of information relating to animals, including several live Webcams to watch animals at the zoo.

www.soselephants.org
This is one of several sites highlighting the issue of ivory poaching. Read here about the problem and what people are doing to fight it.

www.reptilesmagazine.com
The site of this national magazine about reptiles includes information on keeping them as pets, including geckos and other small lizards.

learn.genetics.utah.edu
The University of Utah posted this large site for genetics information, including how traits are passed on in humans and other animals.

Series Glossary of Key Terms

alleles   different forms of a gene; offspring inherit one allele from each parent

chromosomes   molecules within an organism which contain DNA

climate change   the ongoing process in which the temperature of the Earth is growing over time

force   in science, strength or energy that comes as a result of a physical movement or action

frequency   number of waves that pass a given point in a certain period of time

friction   the resistance encountered when an object rubs against another object or on a surface

gene   molecular unit of heredity of living organisms

gravity   the force that pulls objects toward the ground

greenhouse gases   gases in the atmosphere that trap radiation from the sun

inertia   tendency of an object to resist change in motion

laser   an intensified beam of light

lift   the force that acts to raise a wing or an airfoil

momentum   the amount of motion by a moving object

semiconductor a substance that has a conductivity between that of an insulator and that of most metals

sustainable   able to be maintained at a certain rate or level

traits   characteristics of an organism that are passed to the next generation

wavelength   a measurement of light that is the distance from the top of one wave to the next

Picture Credits

Dollarphoto.com: Julija Sapic 8; 22; Goldencoinz 24

Dreamstime.com: Swisshippo 10; Lukaves 13; Onizuka 14; Vandenbroek29 16; Ababaka 18; Isselee 20; Tsombosalexis 21; Outdoorsman 25; Aigarsr 26; Linncurrie 30; Carolyne 31; Jolijuli 33; Snapgalleria 34; Domdeen 36; Parushin 37; Steveheap 38; Bormotov 39; Sloth92 40; Peternasty 41; Corepics 42

ExoTerra: 32

National Library of Medicine: 17

Newscom: Sara-Jane Poole 29

Shutterstock: Moments by Millineux 28

About the Author

Jane P. Gardner has written more than a dozen books for young and young-adult readers on science and other nonfiction topics. She became an author after a career as a science educator. She lives in Massachusetts with her husband, two sons, plus a cat and a gecko!

About the Consultant

Russ Lewin has taught physics, robotics, astronomy, and math at Santa Barbara Middle School in California for more than 25 years. His creative and popular classes and curriculum include a hands-on approach to learning and exploring that instills a love of science in his students.

INDEX

adaptations 16, 17, 18, 20, 21
alpacas 24, 25
amphibians 20, 21
ants 32, 33
Bernoulli, Daniel 14
birds 12-13, 14, 41, 42
boa 20, 21
butterflies 33, 34
cats 8-9
cicadas 38
conditioning 17, 18
crickets 8, 36, 37
dinosaurs 22
dogs 16, 17, 24
eggs 21, 22
elephants 28
extinction 41
feathers 41, 42
flight 12
food web 32, 33

frogs 33
geckos 8, 36
genetics 8-9, 10
grasshoppers 33
Gulf of Mexico 41
hydrothermal vents 34
lift 13, 14
macaw 12-13, 14
Mendel, Gregor 10
Pavlov, Ivan 17
Peru 24
physics 12-13, 25, 37
poaching 28, 29, 30
polar bears 25
Punnett square 10
reptiles 20, 21
rhinoceros 30
sharks 29, 30
temperature 25, 36, 37
whales 25